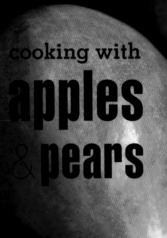

cooking with
apples
& pears

cooking with **apples & pears**

Laura Washburn

photography by Peter Cassidy

RYLAND
PETERS
& SMALL

LONDON NEW YORK

For I.P.

Design, prop styling and photographic art direction Steve Painter
Commissioning Editor Julia Charles
Production Controller Maria Petalidou
Art Director Leslie Harrington
Publishing Director Alison Starling

Food Stylist Linda Tubby
Index Hilary Bird

Author's acknowledgements
Thanks to everyone at Ryland, Peters & Small for putting together such a winning team. The photos, props and food styling are stupendous. Thank you Julia for all your hard work and thanks, as always, Steve, Peter and Linda for such pretty photos. And thank you, Clara and Julian.

First published in the United Kingdom in 2009
by Ryland Peters & Small
20–21 Jockey's Fields
London WC1R 4BW
www.rylandpeters.com

Text © Laura Washburn 2009
Design and photographs
© Ryland Peters & Small 2009

ISBN: 978 1 84597 901 0

10 9 8 7 6 5 4 3 2

A CIP record for this book is available from the British Library.

Printed in China

Notes
• All spoon measurements are level unless otherwise specified.
• Eggs used in the recipes in this book are medium unless specified otherwise.
• Ovens should be preheated to the specified temperatures. All ovens work slightly differently. We recommend using an oven thermometer and suggest you consult the maker's handbook for any special instructions, particularly if you are cooking in a fan-assisted oven, as you will need to adjust temperatures according to manufacturer's instructions.
• To sterilize jars, wash well in soapy water, rinse thoroughly, then boil in plenty of water for 10 minutes. They should be filled as soon as they are dry, and still hot. (If the preserve is cold, let the jar cool before filling.) For further information on preserving visit: http://hgic.clemson.edu/food.htm

contents

introduction

There is possibly no better subject for a cookery book than apples. They are universally liked, and have an amazing range of both sweet and savoury possibilities. There are so many varieties that they offer the cook endless opportunity for experimentation. Apples are available year round and they feature prominently in many cuisines, so there is a wealth of traditional recipes to draw from.

While there are so many different types of apple, the simplest distinction is to separate into eating and cooking apple. The latter tend to be thick skinned and tart – too tart to eat almost – and often disintegrate when cooked. Eating apples are crunchy and sweet, but often lose their flavour when cooked. The most important thing is to learn about the varieties that are local to you and experiment. Quite often, the best choice is not a single type, but a combination of two or three different apples. And, depending on where you live, you might find that the supermarket isn't the only place to find apples. One thing I discovered working on the recipes for this book is that so many people I know have apple trees. Suddenly, I found myself drowning in bags full of luscious home-grown apples from everyone's gardens. It was wonderful.

And alongside apples, there are some pear recipes as these autumnal orchard fruits have so much in common. When it comes to choosing, the same goes for types of pears; it is best to discover what is grown local to you and experiment, as varieties are abundant and all offer different flavours and textures.

But the best part about cooking with apples and pears is the smell. It is warming, comforting and enticing. There is possibly nothing better than the aroma of orchard fruit baking in the oven. Go on, try a recipe or two and see for yourself.

savouries

pear and parmesan salad with endive and walnuts

600 g Belgian endives (about 4–5), cored, halved and very thinly sliced

2 ripe pears, such as Williams, cored and thinly sliced

75–100 g Parmesan cheese, shaved

75 g walnuts, chopped

a handful of flat leaf parsley, finely chopped

For the vinaigrette

2 tablespoons cider vinegar

1 teaspoon fine sea salt

1 teaspoon Dijon mustard

7 tablespoons sunflower oil

1 tablespoon walnut oil (optional)

freshly ground black pepper

Serves 4

An ideal starter, this brings together some lovely seasonal ingredients. To obtain really thin slices of cheese, buy a chunk of Parmesan cheese and use a vegetable peeler. You can find Parmesan shavings in larger supermarkets, but it is often more costly and the flavour is not as good.

First, prepare the vinaigrette. Put the vinegar in a bowl. Using a fork or a small whisk, stir in the salt until almost dissolved. Stir in the mustard. Stir in the oil, a tablespoon at a time, whisking well between each addition, until emulsified. (Note: If you're using the walnut oil, use 1 less tablespoon sunflower oil.) Add pepper to taste.

Just before you're ready to serve the salad, put the salad ingredients in a bowl, pour over the vinaigrette and toss gently with your hands. Divide between serving plates and serve.

1 bunch of watercress, stems trimmed, leaves rinsed and dried

2 red or green apples, such as Gala or Granny Smith, halved, cored and thinly sliced

1 fennel bulb, halved and thinly sliced

75 g Roquefort cheese, crumbled

a handful of flat leaf parsley, finely chopped

a small bunch of chives, snipped

2 cooked beetroot, sliced

For the vinaigrette

2 tablespoons red or white wine vinegar

1 teaspoon fine sea salt

1 teaspoon Dijon mustard

7 tablespoons sunflower oil

1 tablespoon crème fraîche

freshly ground black pepper

Serves 4

apple, beetroot and fennel salad with roquefort

This is a colourful combination of crisp ingredients that will liven up any meal. The mix of flavours and textures is very pleasing; if fennel is unavailable, you could substitute thinly sliced celery.

First, prepare the vinaigrette. Put the vinegar in a bowl. Using a fork or a small whisk, stir in the salt until almost dissolved. Stir in the mustard. Stir in the oil, a tablespoon at a time, whisking well between each addition, until emulsified. Finally, stir in the crème fraîche and add pepper to taste.

Just before you're ready to serve the salad, tear the watercress into pieces and put it in a bowl with the apples, fennel, cheese, parsley and chives. Pour over all but 2 tablespoons of the vinaigrette and toss gently with your hands. Divide the salad between serving plates and top each portion with some beetroot. Drizzle the remaining vinaigrette over the top of each and serve.

500 g red cabbage (about ½ a cabbage), thinly sliced

3 tablespoons red or white wine vinegar or raspberry vinegar

¼ teaspoon fine sea salt

500 g white cabbage (about ½ a cabbage), thinly sliced

125 g grated carrot

1 large tart apple, such as Granny Smith, peeled, cored and coarsely grated

75 g pumpkin seeds, toasted

For the dressing

freshly squeezed juice of ½ an orange

1 tablespoon cider vinegar

½ teaspoon fine sea salt

1 teaspoon sugar

1 tablespoon vegetable oil

180 g natural yoghurt

180 g crème fraîche

freshly ground black pepper

Serves 6—8

apple coleslaw

Plastic tubs of coleslaw are really no match for the real thing and, if you like it but have never made it yourself, you simply must. This recipe has a light creamy dressing and derives its sweetness from the apple, which makes for a delicious and healthy change.

Put the red cabbage in a heatproof bowl. Heat the wine vinegar in a small saucepan until just boiling. Stir in the salt, then pour the mixture over the red cabbage. Toss well. This helps to set the colour.

In a serving bowl, combine the red cabbage, white cabbage, carrot and apple and toss well to combine.

To prepare the dressing, put the orange juice, vinegar, salt and sugar in a small bowl and use a fork or small whisk to mix. Add the oil, yoghurt and crème fraîche. Mix well and season to taste with pepper.

Pour the dressing over the cabbage mixture and toss well. Taste for seasoning and adjust if necessary – it may need more salt, or more vinegar. Refrigerate for several hours before serving. When ready to serve, sprinkle with toasted pumpkin seeds. This is best eaten on the day it is prepared.

1 small onion, chopped

2 tablespoons olive oil

1 teaspoon mild curry powder

a few sprigs of fresh thyme

450 g parsnips (about 2–3), peeled and chopped

1 large tart cooking apple, such as Bramley's, peeled, cored and roughly chopped

1.25 litres chicken or vegetable stock

1 tablespoon unsalted butter

3 heaped tablespoons crème fraîche, plus extra to serve

croûtons, to serve (optional)

sea salt and freshly ground black pepper

Serves 4

apple, parsnip and thyme soup

Parsnips have a very distinctive taste which marries well with the sweetness of apples. In this delicious soup, the two are enhanced by a pinch of spicy curry powder and some fresh thyme. Just the thing to brighten up a dreary winter's day.

Put the onions, oil, curry powder and a good pinch of salt in a large saucepan. Cook gently over low heat until the onions are soft. Add the thyme, parsnips and apple and stir well. Cook for about 5 minutes, adding a little more oil if it needs it and stirring often. Add the stock and season to taste.

Simmer gently, uncovered, until the parsnips are soft, about 15–20 minutes. Purée the soup with a hand-held immersion blender, or by transferring it to a food processor and returning to the saucepan once blended. Taste and adjust the seasoning if necessary.

Stir in the butter and 3 heaped tablespoons crème fraîche and mix well. Ladle the soup into serving bowls and top with croûtons (if using) and a small dollop of crème fraîche.

bakes

pear and chocolate muffins

Pears have the fortunate ability to partner chocolate possibly better than any other fruit. In this recipe they snuggle up to lots of dark chocolate and tangy cream cheese, and some cinnamon adds a pleasing spiciness.

100 g dark chocolate, broken into pieces

100 g unsalted butter

200 g caster sugar

200 g cream cheese (not low-fat)

2 eggs

200 g plain flour

1½ teaspoons baking powder

1 teaspoon ground cinnamon

a pinch of fine sea salt

400 g ripe pears (about 2–3), such as Williams, peeled, cored and diced

100 g dark chocolate chips

a 12-hole muffin tin, lined with paper cases or muffin wrappers

Makes 12 muffins

Preheat the oven to 190°C (375°F) Gas 5.

Put the chocolate and butter in a heatproof bowl and set it over a large saucepan of simmering water – do not let the bottom of the bowl touch the water. Stir gently as it melts. Remove the bowl from the heat just before it has melted completely and allow it to finish melting in the residual heat. Set aside until needed.

Combine the sugar and cream cheese in a mixing bowl. Beat with a hand-held electric whisk until well blended. Add the eggs and melted chocolate mixture and continue beating until well blended.

Combine all the dry ingredients in a separate bowl and mix well. Tip into the chocolate mixture and, with the whisk on low, mix until just blended. Fold in the pears and chocolate chips. Spoon the mixture into the paper cases, dividing it evenly.

Bake in the preheated oven until a skewer inserted in the centre of a muffin comes out almost clean, about 20–30 minutes. Transfer to a wire rack and let cool before serving.

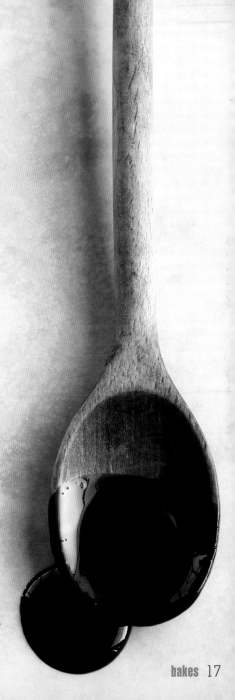

apple spice muffins

140 g plain flour

85 g plain wholemeal flour

145 g dark brown sugar

1 teaspoon bicarbonate of soda

¼ teaspoon baking powder

1 teaspoon ground cinnamon

½ teaspoon each ground nutmeg, ginger and cloves

a pinch of fine sea salt

250 ml buttermilk

125 ml vegetable oil

1 teaspoon vanilla extract

1 tart apple, such as Cox's or Braeburn, peeled, cored and finely chopped

50 g raisins or sultanas

For the frosting

400 g cream cheese (not low-fat)

115 g unsalted butter, softened

120 g icing sugar

1 teaspoon vanilla extract

a 12-hole muffin tin, lined with paper cases or muffin wrappers

Makes 12 muffins

A virtuous mix of apples, raisins, wholemeal flour, buttermilk and loads of warm spices, these muffins are perfect for breakfast, brunch or lunch boxes. If you have fussy children who don't like 'bits', the apple can be coarsely grated and the raisins omitted.

For the frosting, put the cream cheese, butter, sugar and vanilla in a bowl and beat with a hand-held electric whisk until smooth. Refrigerate until needed.

Preheat the oven to 180°C (350°F) Gas 4. In a mixing bowl, combine the plain flour, wholemeal flour, sugar, bicarbonate of soda, baking powder, cinnamon, nutmeg, ginger, cloves and salt. Mix well to combine.

In a separate bowl, combine the buttermilk, oil and vanilla extract. Stir, then add this mixture to the dry ingredients, folding in with a spatula to blend thoroughly. Add the apple and raisins and mix just to combine.

Drop spoonfuls of the mixture into the paper cases, filling each almost to the top. Bake in the preheated oven until puffed and a skewer inserted in the centre of a muffin comes out clean, about 25–35 minutes.

Transfer to a wire rack, let cool completely then spread the top of each muffin with frosting before serving.

apple dappy

This is a traditional British pudding from the West Country, little known, but highly deserving of a larger audience. It is simplicity itself to make using a food processor and uses basic storecupboard ingredients, a few apples and lovely thick clotted cream if you can get some.

450 g tart apples, such as Cox's or Braeburn, peeled, cored and diced

freshly squeezed juice of ½ a lemon

2 tablespoons sugar

1 tablespoon unsalted butter

For the pastry

200 g plain flour

1 teaspoon baking powder

1 teaspoon bicarbonate of soda

a pinch of fine sea salt

60 g unsalted butter

2 tablespoons sugar

2 tablespoons clotted cream or double cream, plus extra to serve

125 ml milk

sugar, for sprinkling

a small square or circular baking tin lined with baking parchment and lightly buttered

Serves 7

Put the apples in a saucepan with the lemon juice, sugar and butter and cook, uncovered, over medium heat until softened. Remove from the heat and set aside.

Preheat the oven to 220°C (425°F) Gas 7.

In a food processor, combine the flour, baking powder, bicarbonate of soda and salt and pulse a few times to blend. Add the butter and sugar and pulse until the mixture resembles fine breadcrumbs. Leave the motor on and add the cream and half of the milk. The dough should be soft and sticky. If it is too stiff, add the remaining milk.

Transfer the dough to a floured surface. You need to roll it out to a 20 x 30 cm rectangle and it should be almost exactly that, not more.

Spread the cooled apple mixture over the dough and roll up from a long end, like a Swiss roll. Mark 7 equal pieces on the roll, then cut into slices using a sharp knife. Arrange the slices, cut-side-up in the baking tin, with one in the centre and the others around it. They should not actually touch as the dough will expand during baking.

Sprinkle generously with sugar and bake in the preheated oven until puffed and golden, about 20–25 minutes. Remove from the oven, let cool slightly, then serve warm with clotted cream.

apple sauce cookies

When I made the Apple Butter on page 62,
I only had a little left; not enough to fill a jar
and too much to throw away. I devised this
recipe as a way to finish it off, which proved
a great success, however jarred apple sauce
works just as well.

50 g unsalted butter, softened

100 g light brown sugar

180 g jarred apple sauce or
Apple Butter (see page 62)

150 g plain flour

½ teaspoon bicarbonate of soda

½ teaspoon baking powder

½ teaspoon ground cinnamon

a pinch of fine sea salt

50 g sultanas or raisins

45 g chopped nuts, such as
walnuts or pecans

*a baking tray, lined with
baking parchment*

Makes 10–12 cookies

Preheat the oven to 200°C (400°F) Gas 6.

Put the butter and sugar in a mixing bowl and beat
together with a hand-held electric whisk until light and
fluffy. Stir in the apple sauce.

In a separate bowl, combine the flour, bicarbonate
of soda, baking powder, cinnamon and salt and mix
well. Add the dry ingredients to the butter mixture and
blend well using a wooden spoon. Add the sultanas
and nuts and fold in.

Drop walnut-sized spoonfuls of the mixture at even
intervals onto the prepared baking tray. Bake in the
preheated oven until the cookies are just golden
around the edges but still soft, about 12–15 minutes.
Transfer to a wire rack to cool. Continue baking in
batches until all the mixture has been used.

The cookies can be stored in an airtight container for
up to 4 days.

apple, fig and nut bars

2 large tart apples, such as
Granny Smith, peeled, cored
and finely chopped

2 tablespoons runny honey

2 tablespoons fresh orange juice

2 tablespoons apple juice
or water

250 g dried figs, finely chopped

375 g plain flour

145 g light brown sugar

250 g unsalted butter, diced

a good pinch of fine sea salt

½ teaspoon ground cinnamon

125 g pecans, hazelnuts, walnuts
or almonds, finely chopped

*a rectangular glass or ceramic
baking dish, 33 x 23 cm, buttered*

Makes 16 bars

**Bars could be described as a bake that falls somewhere
between a tart and soft cookie. This filling is slightly
reminiscent of fig-centred cookies that I ate as a child but
the apples make it lighter. Good for brunch, tea time or
cake sales, or serve warm with ice cream for dessert.**

Preheat the oven to 190°C (375°F) Gas 5.

In a large saucepan, combine the apples, honey, orange and
apple juices. Set over low heat, cover and simmer gently, stirring
occasionally, until tender, about 10–15 minutes. Use a wooden spoon
to help mash the apple pieces. Add the figs and continue simmering,
uncovered, until the figs are soft, about 5 minutes. If necessary, add
more apple juice or water if the mixture seems too thick, and use
a wooden spoon to mash to a coarse purée. Remove from the heat
and set aside to cool.

In a food processor, combine the flour, sugar, butter, salt and
cinnamon. Pulse to obtain coarse crumbs. Alternatively, blend in
a bowl with a pastry cutter, if you have one, or use a palette knife,
then rub in using your fingers to obtain coarse crumbs.

Press half the flour mixture into the bottom of the prepared baking
dish. Spread the apple and fig mixture over the top in an even layer.
Add the nuts to the remaining flour mixture and, using your fingertips,
crumble the mixture over the apples in an even layer.

Bake in the preheated oven until browned, about 30–40 minutes. Let
cool in the baking dish, then cut into bars. The bars will keep in an
airtight container for 7–10 days.

225 g unsalted butter

200 g light brown sugar

6 tablespoons runny honey

275 g plain wholemeal flour

75 g plain flour

2 teaspoons baking powder

1 teaspoon cinnamon

½ teaspoon each ground cloves, ginger and nutmeg

5 eggs, beaten

3 tablespoons ground almonds

50 g sultanas

550 g any tart cooking apples, peeled, cored and finely chopped

4 tablespoons milk

3–4 tablespoons flaked almonds, toasted

icing sugar, for dusting

a cake tin, 23 cm square, buttered and lightly floured

Makes 16 squares

spiced apple cake

This cake hails from Somerset, in England, but as traditional West Country cooking can be a little spartan, I've jazzed up the basic recipe with some honey and spices.

Preheat the oven to 170°C (325°F) Gas 3.

Put the butter and brown sugar in a mixing bowl and cream together until light and fluffy. Beat in the honey. In a separate bowl, combine the flours, baking powder, cinnamon, cloves, ginger and nutmeg.

Fold the dry ingredients into the butter mixture, then add the eggs and mix well using a hand-held electric whisk. Fold in the ground almonds, sultanas, apples and milk and mix just to combine. Transfer the mixture to the prepared tin and level the top.

Bake in the preheated oven until risen and golden and a skewer inserted in the centre of the cake comes out clean, about 50–60 minutes. Let cool slightly in the tin then turn out onto a wire rack. When cool, sprinkle with flaked almonds and dust with icing sugar. Cut into squares to serve. The cake will keep in an airtight container for 4–5 days.

apple and carrot bread with walnuts

250 g plain flour

150 g light muscovado sugar

1 tablespoon baking powder

a pinch of fine sea salt

1 teaspoon ground cinnamon

½ teaspoon ground nutmeg

¼ teaspoon each ground ginger and allspice

100 ml apple juice

75 g unsalted butter, melted

2 large eggs, beaten

1 large tart cooking apple, such as Bramley's, peeled, cored and grated

100 g grated carrots

65 g walnuts, coarsely chopped

a 23 x 13 x 8 cm loaf tin (900 g capacity), buttered

Serves 6–8

This is super simple to make. One large loaf goes a long way and keeps well, so it is ideal if you just want something freshly baked around the house for a few days. It is very nice plain, or spread with butter or cream cheese if you are feeling indulgent. On my testing notes for this recipe, I had scribbled 'yum yum yum'. It says it all!

Preheat the oven to 180°C (350°F) Gas 4.

In a mixing bowl, combine the flour, sugar, baking powder, salt, cinnamon, nutmeg, ginger and allspice. Set aside.

In a separate bowl, mix together the apple juice, melted butter and eggs. Gently fold this mixture into the flour mixture to combine. Use your hands to squeeze every last drop of moisture from the grated apple and carrots then add to the mixture, along with the walnuts and stir just to combine.

Transfer the mixture to the prepared loaf tin and level the top. Bake in the preheated oven until a skewer inserted in the centre of the cake comes out clean, about 1–1¼ hours.

Leave the cake to cool in the tin for a few minutes then turn out onto a wire rack to cool. Slice as you would bread to serve. The cake will keep in an airtight container for 4–5 days.

sweet pastry dough

200 g plain flour
2 teaspoons caster sugar
100 g chilled unsalted butter,
cut into cubes
a pinch of fine sea salt
3–4 tablespoons cold water

*a loose-bottomed tart tin,
about 27 cm diameter,
buttered and lightly floured*

**Makes enough dough for one sweet
pastry case, 27 cm diameter**

**This makes enough for one large tart but the dough freezes
well if carefully wrapped, so I usually make double the
amount while I've got the ingredients out and am getting
the food processor dirty. This way, there is always pastry
dough to hand which is a great time and energy saver.**

Put the flour, sugar, butter and salt in a food processor and, using
the pulse button, process until the mixture is combined (about 5–10
pulses). Add 3 tablespoons water and pulse just until the dough forms
crumbs or holds together; add 1 more tablespoon if it needs it but do
not do more than 10 pulses.

Transfer the dough to a piece of parchment paper, form into a ball
and flatten to a circle. Wrap in the paper and let stand in a cool place
for 30–60 minutes before rolling out.

Roll out the dough on a floured work surface to a circle slightly larger
than the prepared tart tin. Carefully transfer the dough to the tin,
patching any holes as you go and pressing gently into the sides.
The sides should be slightly thicker than the bottom, but only slightly.
To trim the edges, roll a rolling pin over the top, using the edge of the
tin as a cutting surface and let the excess fall away. Tidy up the edges
and refrigerate the pastry case until firm, at least 30 minutes.

To bake blind, preheat the oven to 200°C (400°F) Gas 6. Prick the pastry
base all over, line with parchment paper and fill with baking weights
or dried beans. Bake on a low shelf in the oven for 15 minutes, then
remove the paper and weights and bake until just golden, about
10–15 minutes more. Let the pastry case cool slightly before filling.

tarts and pies

apple tart

1 part-baked sweet pastry case, 27 cm diameter (see Sweet Pastry Dough, page 30)

3 mild eating apples, such as Golden Delicious, peeled, cored and sliced

1 tablespoon unsalted butter, melted

1 tablespoon sugar

sweetened crème fraîche, whipped cream or vanilla ice cream, to serve

For the apple and vanilla purée

3 apples (any variety), peeled, cored and diced

1 vanilla pod, split lengthways

2–4 tablespoons sugar, amount depends on tartness of apples

2 teaspoons unsalted butter

Serves 6–8

Apple tart is a classic but this recipe represents a slight departure. The combination of apples and vanilla is divine so I have added a layer of vanilla-scented apple purée. Serve warm or at room temperature with sweetened crème fraîche, whipped cream or vanilla ice cream.

To make the apple purée, put the diced apples, vanilla pod, sugar and butter in a saucepan with 3–4 tablespoons water. Cook gently, stirring often until soft, adding more water if necessary, about 10–15 minutes. Use the tip of a small knife to scrape the seeds out of the vanilla pod, then discard the pod. Transfer the mixture to a food processor, blender or food mill and purée until smooth.

Preheat the oven to 190°C (375°F) Gas 5. Spread the purée evenly in the pastry case. Carefully arrange the apple slices in a neat circle around the edge; they should be slightly overlapping but not completely squashed together. Repeat to create an inner circle, trimming the slices slightly so that they fit, going in the opposite direction from the outer circle. Brush with melted butter and sprinkle over the sugar.

Bake in the preheated oven until just browned and tender, about 25–35 minutes. Serve warm or at room temperature with sweetened crème fraîche, whipped cream or vanilla ice cream.

tarte tatin

1 recipe Sweet Pastry Dough
(see page 30)

150 g unsalted butter

150 g caster sugar

1.5 kg (about 9) Golden Delicious
or tart apples such as Cox's,
peeled, cored and quartered

crème fraîche, to serve

*a heavy flameproof tart tatin pan
(ideally enamelled cast iron or
lined copper), 20 cm diameter*

Serves 6

Which apple variety to use for a Tarte Tatin is the source of much debate. I like to use Golden Delicious, because they hold their shape well and the mild flavour complements the rich caramel. Others prefer a tart variety, but the important thing is to use one that holds up to cooking. I can't imagine serving this with anything other than crème fraîche.

Roll out the pastry on a floured work surface to a round the diameter of the pan; turn the pan upside-down on the rolled out dough and trace around it with the tip of a sharp knife. Transfer the pastry round to a baking tray and chill until needed.

Put the butter and sugar in the tart tatin pan and set over high heat. Melt, stirring continuously to blend. Remove from the heat and arrange the apple quarters in the pan in 2 circles. The inner circle should go in the opposite direction to the outer circle.

Return to the heat and cook for about 30 minutes. From this point, watch the apples carefully and cook for a further 5–15 minutes, until the liquid thickens and turns a golden caramel colour.

Preheat the oven to 200°C (400°F) Gas 6.

Remove the pan from the heat and top with the pastry round, gently tucking in the edges. Transfer to the preheated oven and bake until browned, about 45–60 minutes. Remove from the oven and let cool only slightly. Unmould while still warm or the caramel will harden making it too difficult. To do this, carefully invert the tart onto a serving plate so that the pastry is on the bottom. Serve hot, warm or at room temperature with crème fraîche.

pear and almond tart

This is a classic French pastry. Sometimes the pears are simply halved, but I think it looks more attractive if they are sliced. Vanilla ice cream or custard sauce are the best partners, but whipped cream or crème fraîche are good too.

1 part-baked sweet pastry case, 27 cm diameter (see Sweet Pastry Dough page 30) or 35 x 11 cm, as shown here

100 g unsalted butter, softened

100 g sugar

2 large eggs

100 g ground almonds

2 tablespoons plain flour

seeds from ½ a vanilla pod split lengthways, or 1 teaspoon vanilla extract

3–4 ripe pears, such as Williams, peeled, cored and sliced

vanilla ice cream or custard sauce, to serve

Serves 6

Preheat the oven to 190°C (375°F) Gas 5.

In a mixing bowl, combine the butter and sugar and beat with a hand-held electric whisk until light and fluffy. Add the eggs one at a time, beating well with each addition. Add the almonds, flour and vanilla seeds and mix just to combine.

Spread the almond mixture in the pastry case in an even layer. Arrange the pear slices on top.

Bake in the preheated oven until puffed and golden, about 20–25 minutes. Serve warm with vanilla ice cream or custard sauce.

dutch apple pie

500 g ready-made shortcrust pastry (thawed if frozen)

1.3 kg tart eating apples, such as Cox's or Braeburn

100 g sugar

100 g sultanas

1 teaspoon ground cinnamon

1 tablespoon freshly squeezed lemon juice

whipped cream, to serve

For the streusel topping

90 g light brown sugar

45 g plain flour

120 g unsalted butter, chilled

1 teaspoon each cinnamon, nutmeg and allspice

a pinch of fine sea salt

80 g walnuts, chopped

a springform cake tin, 24 cm diameter, buttered and floured

Serves 6—8

There are several different ways to top this alternative to a classic American apple pie, including a lattice crust or this streusel topping, which is not strictly speaking Dutch as it comes from the Amish communities of America.

Preheat the oven to 180°C (350°F) Gas 4.

Roll out the pastry on a floured work surface and line the tin with the pastry, all the way up the sides to the top edge. Let chill. Refrigerate while you prepare the apples.

Peel, core and dice the apples and put them in a bowl. Add the sugar, sultanas, cinnamon and lemon juice and mix well using your hands.

In a food processor, combine all the topping ingredients, except the walnuts, and process to form coarse crumbs. Add the walnuts and pulse just a few times to combine.

Put the apple mixture in the pastry-lined tin. Sprinkle the streusel topping over the top in an even layer, going all the way to the edges and tidy up the edges of the pastry.

Cover with foil and bake in the preheated oven for about 30 minutes. Remove the foil and continue baking until the top of the pie is golden, about 25–30 minutes.

Remove from the oven and let cool. Serve warm with whipped cream.

1.3 kg mixed apples, such as Cox's, Braeburn and Golden Delicious, peeled and cored

50 g sugar, or more to taste

1 teaspoon ground cinnamon

1 tablespoon freshly squeezed lemon juice

pouring cream, to serve

For the pastry

300 g plain flour

1 teaspoon sugar

¼ teaspoon fine sea salt

75 g unsalted butter

75 g lard or vegetable shortening

1 egg yolk

4 tablespoons cold water

1 egg, beaten

sugar, for sprinkling

a pie dish or plate (with sloping sides), 23–25 cm diameter, buttered

Serves 6–8

classic apple pie

Apple pie afficionados (me included) believe that the best pies are made with a variety of apples to combine sweet and tart flavours with firm and melting textures.

To make the pastry, put the flour, sugar and salt in a food processor and process just to combine. Add the butter and lard and process using the pulse button until the mixture just forms coarse crumbs. Add the egg yolk and water and pulse again; the mixture should be crumbly but not holding together.

Transfer to a floured work surface and form into a ball. Cut in half, wrap well in clingfilm and chill for at least 1 hour (if leaving longer, double wrap as the dough dries out easily). Roll out one dough half and use to line the bottom of the pie dish. Trim the edges leaving a 1 cm overhang and save the pastry trimmings for decoration if liked. Chill while you prepare the apples.

Cut the apples into slices; not too thick and not too thin. Put them in a bowl with the sugar, cinnamon and lemon juice and use your hands to mix well. Transfer to the dough-lined pie dish.

Preheat the oven to 190°C (375°F) Gas 5.

Roll out the remaining dough on a floured work surface to a circle large enough to cover the apples. Brush the edges of the dough in the dish with beaten egg, then lay the other pastry circle on top. Fold over the overhang from the bottom layer and crimp using your fingertips, or use the tines of a fork to seal. Decorate as desired (a few leaves are traditional) and brush lightly with egg, then sprinkle with sugar. Cut 6–8 small slits in the top of the pie.

Put on a baking tray and bake in the preheated oven until golden, about 50–60 minutes. Serve warm with chilled cream.

praline apple strudel

Praline powder is one of my favourite 'secret' ingredients. It's a cinch to prepare and makes a great addition to many desserts – apple or otherwise. Here it teams up with the crispy flaky filo pastry to lift what would be an ordinary strudel well above the average.

450 g tart eating apples, such as Cox's or Braeburn, peeled, cored and chopped

75 g dried fruit, such as sultanas, cranberries or sour cherries

100 g light brown sugar

1 teaspoon ground cinnamon

1 tablespoon unsalted butter

6 sheets filo pastry (thawed if frozen)

50 g unsalted butter, melted

icing sugar, to dust

whipped cream or crème fraîche, to serve

For the praline

75 g shelled pecans

40 g caster sugar

a baking tray lined with baking parchment

Serves 6–8

To make the praline, combine the pecans and sugar in a non-stick heavy-based frying pan and cook over medium/high heat, stirring constantly, until the sugar hardens and coats the nuts. Transfer to a plate to cool, then process in a coffee grinder or small food processor until ground to a coarse powder. Set aside.

In a large saucepan, combine the apples, dried fruit, brown sugar, cinnamon and 1 tablespoon butter. Cook over medium heat until the apples are soft and the juices have evaporated, about 15 minutes. Remove from the heat and let cool.

Preheat the oven to 190°C (375°F) Gas 5.

Put 2 sheets of filo on the prepared baking tray and brush with some melted butter. Sprinkle with a little praline. Top with 2 more sheets of filo and repeat. Top with 2 more sheets of filo. Spread the apple mixture in an even layer over the top sheet of filo. Sprinkle with more praline mixture, then carefully roll up from a long end, like a Swiss roll. Use the paper to help you roll, if necessary. The seam side needs to be on the bottom. Brush with a little more melted butter, sprinkle with any remaining praline and bake in the preheated oven until crisp and golden, about 25–35 minutes.

Remove from the oven and let cool slightly. Dust with a little icing sugar, slice and serve warm with whipped cream or crème fraîche.

43

desserts

apple and blackberry crumble

There is no better partner for apples than ripe, juicy blackberries.
This easy dessert is simply divine served warm from the oven
with a scoop of vanilla ice cream. If there's any leftover, have it
with yoghurt for breakfast!

900 g mixed apple varieties, peeled,
cored and chopped

450 g blackberries

50 g caster sugar

vanilla ice cream, to serve

For the crumble topping

80 g porridge oats

140 g plain flour

80 g light brown sugar

80 g ground almonds

½ teaspoon ground cinnamon

150 g unsalted butter, cut into cubes

*an ovenproof dish, 23–25 cm
diameter or 4–6 individual dishes,
9–12 cm diameter, well-buttered*

Serves 4–6

Preheat the oven to 200°C (400°F) Gas 6.

Put the apples, berries and sugar in a mixing bowl and use your hands to
mix well. Transfer to the prepared baking dish.

To prepare the crumble topping, combine the oats, flour, sugar, almonds
and cinnamon in a bowl and mix well. Add the butter. Using a pastry
blender, or your fingertips, rub in the butter until the mixture resembles
coarse breadcrumbs. Alternatively, use a food processor and blend carefully
with the pulse button; do not over-process or you will grind the oats too finely.

Sprinkle the topping evenly over the apple mixture. Bake in the preheated
oven until the crumble is golden and the fruit is bubbling, about 35–45
minutes. Serve warm with vanilla ice cream.

apple brown betty with dried cranberries

900 g tart apples, such as Cox's or Granny Smith, peeled, cored and diced

1 teaspoon ground cinnamon

1 tablespoon finely grated orange zest

75 ml apple or orange juice

100 g dried cranberries

375 g fresh white breadcrumbs

85 g unsalted butter, melted

80 g shelled pecans, chopped

75 g light brown sugar

2 tablespoons unsalted butter

whipped cream, to serve

a non-stick baking dish, about 20 cm diameter, well-buttered

Serves 4–6

This is another traditional American recipe with very humble origins. It is always made with apples but not necessarily dried cranberries. Just like English bread pudding, it is an economic way to use up stale bread but I have found that it tastes even better if you use fresh white bread or even brioche.

Preheat the oven to 190°C (375°F) Gas 5.

In a bowl, combine the apples, cinnamon, orange zest, apple juice and cranberries. Toss gently with your hands to mix and set aside.

In a separate bowl, combine the breadcrumbs and melted butter and mix well.

Spread about one-third of the buttered breadcrumbs in the bottom of the prepared baking dish. Add the pecans and sugar to the remaining breadcrumbs and mix to combine.

Put half of the apple mixture on top of the breadcrumbs in the baking dish. Top with half the breadcrumb and pecan mixture and top this with the remaining apple mixture and finish with the remainder of the breadcrumb and pecan mixture. Dot with 2 tablespoons butter and bake in the preheated oven until golden, about 30–40 minutes. Serve warm with whipped cream.

pear cobbler

900 g pears, peeled, cored and sliced

75 g light brown sugar

2 tablespoons plain flour

1 teaspoon vanilla extract

finely grated zest of 1 orange

vanilla ice cream or whipped cream, to serve

For the cobbler batter

300 g plain flour

200 g sugar

1 tablespoon baking powder

a pinch of fine sea salt

250 ml milk

125 g unsalted butter, melted

extra sugar or cinnamon sugar, to sprinkle

an ovenproof baking dish, about 23–25 cm diameter, well-buttered

Serves 4–6

A cobbler is a dessert consisting of a sweetened thick batter poured over fruit and baked. Other names for similar recipes are grunt, slump and buckle, but they are all pretty much the same thing. It is a homely dish, easy to make and even easier to eat!

Preheat the oven to 190°C (375°F) Gas 5.

In a bowl, combine the pears, sugar, flour, vanilla extract and orange zest. Toss gently with your hands to combine and arrange in an even layer in the bottom of the prepared baking dish. Set aside.

To prepare the cobbler batter, combine the flour, sugar, baking powder and salt in a separate bowl. In a third bowl, stir together the milk and melted butter. Gradually pour the milk mixture into the dry ingredients, beating with a wooden spoon until just smooth.

Drop spoonfuls of the batter on top of the pears, leaving gaps but spreading to the edges. Sprinkle the top with sugar and bake in the preheated oven until golden brown, about 40–50 minutes. Serve warm with vanilla ice cream or whipped cream.

pear and fig clafoutis with almonds

3 ripe pears
3 ripe figs
200 ml crème fraîche
200 ml milk
3 eggs
125 g sugar
2 tablespoons ground almonds
⅛ teaspoon ground cinnamon
icing sugar, to dust
pouring cream, to serve

*a non-stick baking dish, about
22–25 cm diameter, well-buttered*

Serves 4–6

This delicious dessert is ideal for entertaining because it looks fantastic but is very easy to prepare. Simply make the batter and prepare the fruit in advance, then combine the two and put in the oven at the start of the meal. It will be done just when you are ready to serve.

Preheat the oven to 200°C (400°F) Gas 6.

Peel and core the pears and cut into largeish pieces. Trim the stem ends from the figs and cut into slightly smaller pieces. If there is too much white on the skins, trim this off. Put the fruit in the prepared baking dish and distribute evenly. Set aside.

In a mixing bowl, combine the crème fraîche, milk, eggs, sugar, almonds and cinnamon. Mix well with a hand-held electric whisk.

Pour the batter evenly over the fruit and bake in the preheated oven until puffed and golden, about 35–45 minutes. Let cool slightly and dust with icing sugar just before serving. Serve warm with chilled pouring cream.

2 apples, preferably Cox's or Braeburn

1 just-ripe pear, preferably Conference

20 g hazelnuts, coarsely chopped

1 tablespoon sultanas

4–5 dried apricots, chopped

ground cinnamon, to dust

about 1–2 oz. unsalted butter

runny honey, to drizzle

natural Greek yoghurt, to serve

a non-stick baking dish, large enough to comfortably hold the fruit

Serves 2

baked apples and pears with dried fruit, honey and hazelnuts

Baked fruit is both easy on the cook and easy on the waistline. This recipe gives quantities for two servings to make it simple to increase as needed. I like to serve these with a dollop of natural, unsweetened Greek yoghurt.

Preheat the oven to 200°C (400°F) Gas 6.

Peel the apples. If necessary, trim the bottoms slightly so that they sit flat. Using a small knife or a corer, remove the cores. With a small spoon, scrape out some apple around the core cavity to allow for more stuffing. Peel the pear, halve and scoop out the core, as for the apple.

In a small bowl, mix together the hazelnuts, sultanas and apricots.

Arrange the apples and pears in the baking dish. Stuff the nut mixture into the apple and pear cavities, mounding it at the top. Top each with a light sprinkling of cinnamon and a good knob of butter, then drizzle each with 1–2 teaspoons of honey, to taste. Cover with foil.

Bake in the preheated oven for 20 minutes, then remove the foil and continue baking until just golden, about 10–15 minutes. Divide the apples and pears carefully between serving plates and pour over any pan juices. Serve warm with natural Greek yoghurt.

poached pears

These glistening crimson pears make a lovely simple ending to a rich meal. They are a very good choice for entertaining as they should be made in advance so that they have time to marinate in the poaching liquid and take on their gorgeous jewel-like colour.

In a saucepan large enough to hold the pears standing upright, combine the wine, sugar, honey, lemon juice, cinnamon stick, vanilla pod, orange peel, clove and peppercorn. Warm over low heat, stirring occasionally until the sugar has dissolved. Remove from the heat.

Peel the pears but leave them whole.

Place the pears in the wine mixture and simmer, uncovered, until tender (test with the tip of a sharp knife). Timing depends on the quantity, size and ripeness of the pears, about 20–35 minutes.

Transfer the pears to a shallow, non-reactive bowl using a large slotted spoon. Continue cooking the poaching liquid over medium heat until it has reduced by half. Let cool, then strain it through a sieve and pour over the pears. Leave the pears in the liquid, turning them occasionally, for at least 3 hours before serving.

Note: This dessert can be made up to several days in advance and kept refrigerated. Return the pears to room temperature before serving.

750 ml (1 bottle) good red wine
150 g sugar
3 tablespoons runny honey
freshly squeezed juice of 1 lemon
1 cinnamon stick
1 vanilla pod, split lengthways
1 large piece of orange peel
1 whole clove
1 black peppercorn
4–6 firm pears
sweetened crème fraîche, whipped cream or vanilla ice cream, to serve

Serves 4–6

300 g genoese sponge (about one 23–25 cm cake)

4 tablespoons cognac (optional)

4–6 poached pears (see page 55) poaching liquid reserved

250 ml whipping cream, whipped

toasted flaked almonds, to top

For the custard

250 ml milk

50 ml double cream

8 egg yolks

75 g sugar

1 vanilla pod, split lengthways or
1 teaspoon vanilla extract

a glass serving dish or 4–6 individual serving dishes

Serves 4–6

spiced pear trifle

Trifle is a traditional English dessert but this recipe departs from the classic recipe as it uses spiced poached pears instead of tinned peaches. It is easy to make and looks spectacular when assembled in a large glass bowl.

To make the custard, combine the milk and cream in a saucepan and warm over low heat. Meanwhile, whisk together the egg yolks and sugar in a heatproof bowl. Whisk the warm milk mixture into the egg yolk mixture, then return the mixture to the saucepan, stirring constantly with a wooden spoon, until it thickens. As soon as it thickens, remove from the heat, transfer to a bowl and scrap in the vanilla seeds from the pod. Stir them into the custard. Cover the surface of the custard closely with greaseproof paper to prevent a skin from forming and set aside to cool.

When you're ready to serve, cut the sponge cake into pieces and arrange these in the bottom of the serving dish. Drizzle with the cognac (if using) and some reserved pear poaching liquid. Top with the quartered pears, then spoon over some of the custard. Spoon the whipped cream on top, sprinkle with the almonds and serve.

chutneys and jams

chutneys

Home-made chutneys are a great thing to keep on hand. They are ideal served with a selection of cheeses and biscuits, as part of a ploughman's lunch, and they are perfect with roast meats – both hot and cold. They also make a nice sandwich ingredient. The Apple, Pear and Ginger Chutney is especially suited to pork, and the Apple, Red Onion and Dried Cherry Chutney goes very well with chicken, turkey and even duck.

apple, pear and ginger chutney

3 eating apples, such as Golden Delicious, peeled, cored and diced

2 large ripe pears, peeled, cored and diced

1 large white onion, finely chopped

375 ml cider vinegar

350 g light brown sugar

100 g sultanas or raisins

140-g piece of fresh ginger, peeled and finely chopped

½ teaspoon sea salt

½ teaspoon dried red chilli flakes

Makes 1–1.5 litres

In a large non-reactive saucepan, combine the apples, pears, onion, vinegar, sugar, sultanas, ginger, salt and chilli flakes. Cook over medium heat, stirring occasionally, until thick, about 30–40 minutes.

Transfer the chutney to a spotlessly clean and dry, sealable airtight container. It will keep in the fridge for up to 2 weeks.

apple, red onion and dried cherry chutney

3 eating apples, such as Golden Delicious, peeled, cored and diced

1 large or 2 medium red onions, halved and sliced

175 g dried sour cherries

500 ml cider vinegar

3 tablespoons light brown sugar

¼ teaspoon ground cloves

¼ teaspoon sea salt

freshly ground black pepper

Makes 500–750 ml

In a large non-reactive saucepan, combine the apples, onion, dried cherries, vinegar, sugar, cloves, salt and a few grinds of black pepper. Cook over medium heat, stirring occasionally, until thick, about 30–40 minutes.

Transfer the chutney to a spotlessly clean and dry, sealable airtight container. It will keep in the fridge for up to 2 weeks.

roasted pear relish

A fantastic accompaniment to roast pork and poultry or bread with mature Cheddar.

4 ripe pears, peeled, halved and cored
2 tablespoons freshly squeezed lemon juice
1 tablespoon light brown sugar
50 g white granulated sugar
¾ teaspoon ground cinnamon
¼ teaspoon ground cloves
65 ml pure maple syrup
1 small red onion, cut into 1-cm slices
1 tablespoon peeled and grated fresh ginger
5 tablespoons raisins
125 ml cider vinegar
1 teaspoon dried red chilli flakes (optional)
vegetable oil, for brushing

Serves 4–6

Preheat the oven to 180°C (350°F) Gas 4.

Brush a baking tray with vegetable oil. In a bowl, combine the pears, lemon juice, both the sugars, cinnamon and cloves and mix well to coat the pears. Arrange the pears cut-side down on the tray and brush with a little more oil. Roast in the preheated oven until caramelized, about 45 minutes. When the pears are cool enough to handle, cut into small cubes.

Meanwhile, put the remaining ingredients in a non-reactive saucepan and bring to the boil. Reduce the heat and simmer, uncovered, for 5 minutes. Remove from the heat and let cool. Add the cubed pears to the onion mixture and mix well. Cover and refrigerate for at least 1 day before serving. Transfer the relish to a spotlessly clean and dry, sealable airtight container. It will keep in the fridge for up to 10 days.

apple jelly

This is delicious without any flavourings, but adding fresh sage makes it perfect for brushing over pork as it roasts. Elderflower with apple is a quintessentially English combination and worth trying if you are able to find elderflowers when they are in season.

3.5 kg tart cooking apples, such as Bramley's
sugar, as required (see method below)
freshly squeezed juice of 1 lemon, strained
a few fresh sage leaves or untreated elderflowers (optional)

Makes about 3 kg

Slice the apples but do not peel or core. Put the apple slices in a large non-reactive saucepan and add water to cover. Add the elderflowers at this point, if using. Cook over medium heat until soft, about 30–40 minutes, and then let stand overnight.

The next day, prepare a nylon jelly bag or, if you don't have one, boil a tea towel in a large saucepan of water for 2–3 minutes, wring well and leave to cool before using. Set the bag or tea towel over a bowl, pour in the apple mixture and let it slowly drip through; do not stir or squeeze the bag or the jelly will be cloudy.

Measure the juice, then transfer it to a separate clean non-reactive saucepan. Simmer, uncovered, for about 5 minutes, skimming off any foam that rises to the surface. For each 250 ml apple liquid you'll need to add 200–250 g sugar. Stir until dissolved.

Boil until setting point; the jelly will turn a darker amber colour. Stir in the lemon juice and pour into hot, dry sterilized jars (see note on page 4). Add a few sage leaves, if using. Let cool, then seal. The jelly will keep for 3–4 weeks if correctly sealed.

apple and cranberry sauce

This is a classic fruit sauce to accompany turkey, goose or roast pork. A good pinch of ground cloves and a dash of balsamic vinegar during cooking will dress it up for Christmas.

350 g fresh cranberries
1 large tart cooking apple, such as Bramley's, peeled, cored and chopped
60 g dried apricots, chopped
150 g sugar
4 tablespoons freshly squeezed orange juice

Serves 4–6

Combine all the ingredients in a large non-reactive saucepan and cook over medium heat, stirring often. Add a little water if the mixture seems dry. The cranberries will pop as they cook, which is fine.

Cook until the fruit has softened and the mixture is thick, about 15–20 minutes. Remove from the heat. Taste for sweetness; add more sugar if desired. Transfer the sauce to a spotlessly clean and dry, sealable airtight container. It will keep in the fridge for 3–4 days. Bring to room temperature to serve.

apple pumpkin jam

This is an unusual and delicious conserve, and a handy Autumn recipe as it offers a use for retired Halloween jack o'lanterns.

1 kg pumpkin, peeled, deseeded and diced
1 kg tart cooking apples, such as Bramley's, peeled, cored and chopped
freshly squeezed juice of ½ a lemon
500 g sugar
1 teaspoon ground ginger

Makes 1.2 litres

Put all the ingredients in a large non-reactive saucepan. Cook over medium heat, covered, for about 5–10 minutes to release the juices, then remove the lid and lower the heat.

Simmer for 40–50 minutes, stirring occasionally, and mashing the apples and pumpkin with a wooden spoon to break up the bigger pieces.

Let cool, then transfer the jam to a spotlessly clean and dry, sealable airtight container. It will keep in the fridge for up to 10 days.

apple blackberry jam

This fruity jam is unbelievably simple to make but extraordinarily delicious.

600 g blackberries
625 g (about 3) cooking apples, such as Bramley's, peeled, cored and chopped
450 g sugar
1 tablespoon freshly squeezed lemon juice

Makes about 1 litre

Combine the blackberries, apples, sugar and lemon juice in a large non-reactive saucepan. Cook over medium heat, stirring, until the sugar dissolves.

Continue cooking, stirring occasionally, until the fruit softens, about 20–30 minutes. Use a wooden spoon to crush the fruit slightly as you stir. Remove from the heat. Transfer the jam to a spotlessly clean and dry, sealable airtight container. It will keep in the fridge for 7–10 days.

apple butter

This is actually apple jam, but in America it is called Apple Butter. Use it as you would any fruit jam; spread on toast, with brioche, in sandwiches, drizzled over pancakes or as a filling for sponge cakes.

1.5 kg mixed apples, such as Braeburn, Cox's and Bramley's, peeled, cored and chopped
350 g runny honey
200 g sugar
2 tablespoons freshly squeezed lemon juice
1 teaspoon ground cinnamon
½ teaspoon ground cloves
250 ml apple juice

Makes about 2 kg

Combine all the ingredients in a large non-reactive saucepan. Bring to the boil, stirring occasionally. Lower the heat and simmer, stirring occasionally, and using a wooden spoon, crush the apples, until thick, about 20–25 minutes. Remove from the heat.

Transfer the jam to a spotlessly clean and dry, sealable airtight container. It will keep in the fridge for 7–10 days. Alternatively, spoon into hot, dry sterilized jars while hot (see note on page 4). Let cool, then seal. The jam will keep for 3–4 weeks if correctly sealed.

index